HIGHLIGHT 9

Mittelschule Bayern

Workbook

für R-Klassen

 Audios online verfügbar unter go.cornelsen.de.

Code: uway8-pkess

Cornelsen

INHALT

So viele Zeichen im Workbook – was bedeuten sie?

Die Ampel – Wie schwer fällt dir eine Übung?
In der Ampel kannst du markieren, wie schwer dir eine (Teil-)Übung gefallen ist:
rot = schwer, gelb = mittel, grün = leicht.

Leere und volle Kreise – so gut du kannst
Leichtere Aufgaben sind mit einem leeren Kreis markiert und schwierigere mit einem vollen.

Kopfhörer – Audios online
Für diese Angebote brauchst du einen Internetzugang:
Auf *go.cornelsen.de* findest du alle Tonaufnahmen (Audios) im MP3-Format.
Der Zugangscode dafür steht auf der ersten Seite vom Workbook. Die Zahl unter dem Kopfhörer ist die Track-Nummer der Tonaufnahme.

Stift; Partnerarbeit – wie du diese Übungen bearbeiten sollst
Für Aufgaben, neben denen ein Stift abgebildet ist, schreibst du deine Antwort auf ein anderes Blatt Papier. Die Köpfe beziehen sich auf Übungen, die du zu zweit bearbeiten kannst.

Lupe – Suche im Internet
Für diese Aufgabe brauchst du einen Internetzugang um die Informationen online zu finden.

G'day from Australia

1 **Fun facts about Australia**

a Do you know or can you guess the right answers? Tick (✓) a, b oder c.

1 There are **a** ☐ 1,742 **b** ☐ 6,493 **c** ☐ 10,685 beaches in Australia.

2 The land area of Australia is about

   a ☐ the same size as Germany

   b ☐ seven times bigger than Germany

   c ☐ 21 times bigger than Germany.

3 Germany has about 84 million people.
The population of Australia is about ...

   a ☐ 26 million **b** ☐ 57 million

   c ☐ 138 million.

4 This photo of an island in Western Australia shows ...

   a ☐ a huge field of pink roses

   b ☐ the set of a science-fiction film

   c ☐ a natural pink lake.

5 When it is born, a baby kangaroo is about ... long.

   a ☐ 2 cm **b** ☐ 12 cm **c** ☐ 22 cm

6 Wombat poo[1] is special because it's

   a ☐ yellow! **b** ☐ edible[2]! **c** ☐ square[3]!

7 Australia's name comes from the Latin word *australis*
which means ...

   a ☐ beautiful **b** ☐ southern

   c ☐ like Austria **d** ☐ wombat

a wombat

8 About ... of the population in Australia lives on the coast (50 km or less from the sea).

   a ☐ 25% **b** ☐ 45% **c** ☐ 85%

9 How many hours a day does a koala sleep?

   a ☐ 2–5 **b** ☐ 8–12 **c** ☐ 18–22

SB → p.11

b Listen and check your answers. How many did you get right?
02

---

[1]poo Kot [2]edible essbar [3]square quadratisch

2 Staying safe

Complete this article for tourists with words from the box. You don't need all the words.

> between • call • ~~climate~~ • down • drink • jellyfish •
> rely • shade • sick • skin • sting • torch • wear • work

In hot weather

Parts of Australia have a very hot *climate*_____, so it's important to _____ a lot of

water. If you are too hot and feel _____, you should go into the _____ and put

wet towels over your face. And _____ a doctor if you don't get better.

At the beach

Be careful if there are _____ in the water. Swim _____ the flags.

And look after your _____: use good suncream and _____ a hat and T-shirt.

In the outback

Take lots of water, a whistle and a _____ to use at night. If your car breaks _____,

use it for shade. Don't _____ on your phone – it might not _____ in the outback.

SB → p.13

3 SPEAKING 👥 What should I do?

Partner A: Choose a situation. Partner B: Say what your partner should do. Then change roles.
Talk about three situations each.

> I feel hot and sick.

> I have sunburn on my arms.

> My dog looks hot and unhappy.

> I've got a bad jellyfish sting and I feel sick.

> I'm going to the outback.

> I'm going to the beach.

> I'm very, very hot and my throat is dry.

I think you should... (and ...)	stay in the shade drink lots of water wear a shirt / hat
	see a doctor take a torch / whistle give it lots of water
	put on some suncream take lots of water keep it in the shade

Oh, thanks.   Good idea.   I'll do that.

SB → p.13

🎧 **4** **LISTENING** Brolga and his kangaroos
03

Listen to the radio programme.
Section A: tick (✓) the correct answers.
Sections B & C: tick (✓) True or False.
Section D: write the answers.

A 1 Brolga

a) ☐ helps kangaroos and birds

b) ☐ saves baby kangaroos

c) ☐ saves mother kangaroos

d) ☐ takes photos of kangaroos

2 Brolga started in

a) ☐ 2005

b) ☐ 2011

c) ☐ 2014

d) ☐ 2015

3 His first baby kangaroo's mother died

a) ☐ at a bus station

b) ☐ in the town centre

c) ☐ in a river

d) ☐ in a road accident

Chris "Brolga" Barns from the Baby Kangaroo Rescue Centre in Alice Springs

TIP

Remember – the questions sometimes use *different* words from what you hear.

B 1 The name for a baby kangaroo is a joey.　　True ☐　False ☐

2 Brolga has saved over 200 kangaroos.　　True ☐　False ☐

3 Brolga lives in the city.　　True ☐　False ☐

C 1 Brolga has a name for each joey.　　True ☐　False ☐

2 All the kangaroos go back to live in the outback in the end.　　True ☐　False ☐

3 The joeys even go shopping with Brolga.　　True ☐　False ☐

● **D** Visiting the kangaroo centre:

Which days: *Tuesday to* _____

Tours are: _____ *to* _____ *hours*

Price: Adult: $ _____　Child: $ _____

SB → p.13

5 **Europeans and indigenous Australians**
Which people are described? Draw lines.

used boomerangs to hunt animals

brought diseases like the flu

built towns

were the first people in Australia

indigenous Australians

were killed or put in prison

lived in harmony with nature

Europeans in Australia

came to Australia in the 1700s

took the best land for farms

tried to destroy the others' culture

had respect for the environment

SB → p.14

6 **Indigenous Australian culture**
a Write the words with the missing vowels: a, e, i, o, u.

bdy pntng – __ __ __ __ __ __ __ __ __

ddgrds – __ __ __ __ __ __ __ __

sngs – __ __ __ __ __

**indigenous
Australian culture**

strs – __ __ __ __ __

pntngs – __ __ __ __ __ __ __

bmrngs – __ __ __ __ __ __ __ __

trdtnl dnc stps – __ __ __ __ __ __ __ __ __ __ __ __ __ __ __ __

b Circle the right word(s).

1 Life was better / worse for Aboriginals before Europeans came.

2 In Australia now there are more indigenous Australians / white people than indigenous Australians / white people.

3 There are many / no problems for indigenous Australians today.

4 Indigenous culture is not / still strong.

5 The Burdekin Crew are very positive / negative about their culture.

SB → p.15

7 **New words in the story**

Complete the puzzle with new words from the story.

1 Someone you don't know is a …

3 An important test at school

6 Ask for food in a cafe

8 Tell someone what they should do

   = give them some …

10 (Down ↓) 'Uluru' is the traditional,

   indigenous name for this place.

   The British who colonized Australia

   called it: _____

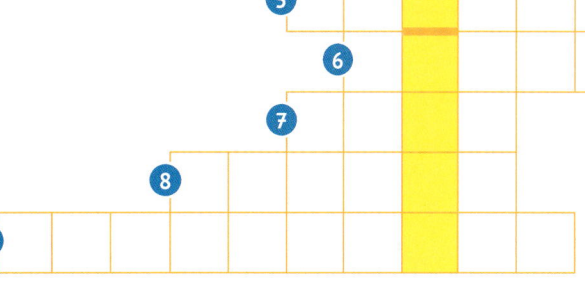

2    4    5    7    9    10

SB → p.18

8 **What do you think?**

What do you think of the story and the characters?
Would you like to read the book?
How many stars do you give the story? (★ → ★★★★★)

> **Here are some ideas:**
> I think   the story is …   the characters are …   very …   too …   and quite …
>   good   exciting   interesting   funny   boring   violent   glamorous   nice
> I would / wouldn't like to read the book because …
> I like / I don't really like   the people in it / that sort of story
> I give this story … stars

SB → p.18

FOCUS

The past progressive

- Mit dem past progressive sagst du, was in der Vergangenheit gerade im Gange war oder im Hintergrund passierte.
  Es besteht aus: was / were + der ing-Form des Verbs. Verneinungen: wasn't / weren't + ing
- Wenn eine neue Handlung dazu kommt, steht diese im simple past.

I was having lunch

when suddenly my phone rang.

The dog ate my lunch

while I was talking on the phone and wasn't looking!

---

9 ⊙ **At the wildlife centre**

Jamie is telling his friend Ruby about his holiday in Australia. Circle the right words.

> TIP
> I / he / she / it... **was / wasn't**
> you / we / they... **were / weren't**

We went to the wildlife centre on our first day. The sun wasn't / weren't shining, but it was hot. I loved the kangaroos. A man was / were feeding them, and they was / were eating from his hand! Some kangaroos wasn't / weren't doing very much. One was / were sleeping on the ground. Two kangaroos was / were jumping around. Mum said they wasn't / weren't fighting – the big one was / were just playing with its friend, it wasn't / weren't hurting the little one. They were really cute!

SB → p.20

---

10 **Jamie and the koala**

Write the verbs in the past progressive.

> TIP
> tak~~e~~ → taking (& smil~~e~~, mak~~e~~)

While we _____ _____ (walk) around, we saw two men who _____ _____

(take) photos of people with koalas. They took my photo, but I _____ _____ (not smile)

because I _____ _____ (start) to feel wet. But it _____ _____ (not rain)

– the koala was peeing[1] on me!! Mum and dad _____ _____ (laugh) so much, they

_____ _____ (make) me feel even more

stupid! I was glad that most people _____

_____ (not look) at me! And at least I _____

_____ (not wear) my favourite T-shirt ...

SB → p.20

---

[1] pee pinkeln

11 On the way to the beach

Jamie talks more about his holiday.
<u>Underline</u> the right verbs:
simple past or past progressive.

TIPP

Gerade im Gange /
im Hintergrund /
while...?

Neue Handlung /
when suddenly ...?

The next day, we decided / were deciding to

go to the beach. While we drove / were driving

there, Dad suddenly stopped / was stopping the car and pointed / was pointing to the side of the road.

There, we saw / were seeing a really huge kangaroo! It stood / was standing beside the road.

But while I looked / was looking for my phone, it suddenly went / was going into the trees, so I

didn't get / wasn't getting a photo.

SB → p.20

12 At the beach

a Write the verbs in the simple past or past progressive.

TIP

get → ge**tt**ing

When we _____ (arrive) at the beach, the sun _____ (shine). While mum

and dad _____ (read) their books, I _____ (go) into the sea. I _____

_____ (enjoy) myself, when suddenly I _____ (see) a huge, dangerous jellyfish! It

_____ (come) towards me. I _____ (shout) for help, but mum and dad _____

_____ (sleep). I _____ (start) to panic because it _____ (get)

nearer! Then I _____ (laugh). It wasn't a dangerous jellyfish – it was a plastic bag!

b Write the verbs in the simple past or past progressive.

TIP

lie → **ly**ing

While I _____ (look) for a bin for the

plastic bag, I _____ (hear) a noise. A little girl

_____ (stand) next to the rubbish bin,

and she _____ (cry) . "A man _____

(take) my phone!" she _____ (tell) me. "He _____

_____ (wear) a red T-shirt. Look – there he

is!!" I _____ (look) over. The man _____ (sit) on a wall and _____

(talk) to a woman. We both _____ (shout), and the man and woman _____ (run)

away. But when we _____ (get) to the wall, the phone _____ (lie) on it!

SB → p.20

13 Opposites

a ⊙ Find the opposites. Write the correct letters in the boxes.

| **1** day | **2** in front of | **3** inside | **4** am |
| **5** before | **6** near | **7** find | **8** down |

| **a** far | **b** after | **c** up | **d** behind |
| **e** pm | **f** lose | **g** night | **h** outside |

1	2	3	4	5	6	7	8

b Write the opposites.

1 left   **2** happy   **3** hot   **4** fast   **5** inside   **6** good

_____   _____   _____   _____   _____   _____

SB → p.22

14 Stars in the jungle¹

Read the text. Tick (✓) the correct options below.

I really like the reality TV shows from the jungle. There are
usually ten or twelve stars who __1__ live in the Australian jungle.
They stay there for __2__ weeks, and have to do different
challenges to get extra food.
I think the __3__ thing of all is when they eat insects² __4__ are
still alive³ – yuk!!! I could __5__ do that – I'd be sick! The people
who do it eat them really __6__ and make funny faces! I don't
like the things they do with spiders and rats – I'm really scared
__7__ them! I've never __8__ to the jungle, but I'd like to go one day.

1	☐ can	☐ have to	☐ mustn't
2	☐ a bit	☐ a little	☐ a few
3	☐ hard	☐ harder	☐ hardest
4	☐ where	☐ which	☐ who
5	☐ never	☐ ever	☐ often
6	☐ quick	☐ quickly	☐ quiet
7	☐ from	☐ of	☐ for
8	☐ be	☐ being	☐ been

TIP

When you've chosen a word,
read the whole sentence. Is it right?

SB → p.22

¹jungle Dschungel   ²insect Insekt   ³alive lebend

15 **Talking to the doctor**

Put the dialogue in the right order. Write the numbers 1 to 12.

☐   Yes, my head is very sore, and I have a temperature.

☐   You should rest. Sleep a lot and drink a lot.

1   G'day. What can I do for you?

☐   What should I do?

☐   Yes, I think it's the flu.

☐   Thanks very much. Goodbye.

☐   I'm not feeling very well, doctor. I have a sore throat.

5   Do your arms and legs hurt?

☐   Yes, you can take painkillers if your headache is bad.

☐   Yes, they do. And I feel very tired too. Do I have the flu?

☐   Open your mouth... Yes, your throat is red. Do you have a headache?

10   Should I take painkillers?

 SB → p.23

16 **LISTENING** **Problems**

Four people have problems! Listen to the dialogues.
Find the right picture and write the letter.

1 ___   2 ___   3 ___   4 ___

> **TIPP**
>
> Bereite dich aufs Hören vor. Schaue dir die Bilder an. Welche englischen Wörter könntest du hören?

A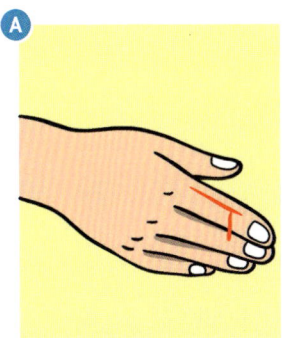

B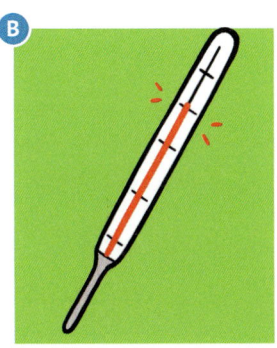

C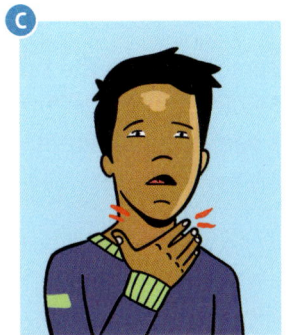

D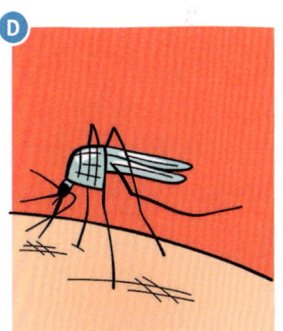

E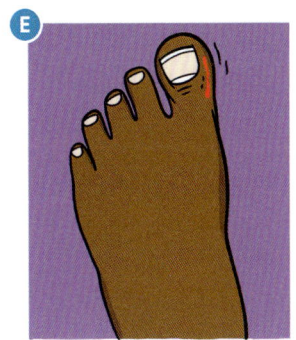

F

G

H

SB → p.23

17 **WRITING** **A holiday**

a You are going to answer Jamie's email. First, read the email.

> Hi there!
> I had a fantastic holiday in Australia. Please tell me about a holiday you had,
> or one day of a holiday. Where were you? What was it like? What did you do there?
> Bye for now
> Jamie

b Prepare to write. These tips will help you write a good text.

> **Step 1:** Read what you have to do and make notes.

• <u>Underline</u> the questions in Jamie's email. Make notes for each question in your exercise book.

> **Step 2:** Use time phrases and linking words, e.g. and, but, so, because.

because • on Sunday
• so • at 1 pm

• Make this text better. Put in words from the box.

It was sunny. We went to the beach. We had lunch. We ate in the car. It started to rain.

_____

_____

> **Step 3:** Don't use the same words all the time.

• Make these sentences better. Use different words:

The holiday was good, and we had good weather. We stayed in a good hotel, where the food was good. The evenings were good because we saw some good shows.

Ideas: sunny • comfortable • amazing • nice • perfect • fun • great • fantastic • brilliant

The holiday was _____

_____

_____

c Write your email in your exercise book. Use the tips to help you. Write about 80 words.

> **Step 4:** Check your work:
> Is the spelling OK? Are the words correct? Have you answered all the questions?

SB → *p.23*

Das kann ich auf Englisch!
Hier kannst du überprüfen, ob und wie gut du alles verstanden hast. Finde auch heraus, wo du dich noch verbessern kannst. Was kannst du schon sehr gut ● oder recht gut ●? Was musst du noch üben ●? Male die Ampellichter entsprechend aus.

Unit 1

1 **Ich kann meine Meinung darlegen und begründen.**
• Write about a good film that you've seen. Complete the sentences.

1 A good film that I have seen is _____.

2 I think the story is _____.

3 The characters are _____.

4 I give this film _____ stars.

5 I really liked this film because _____.

WB → S.7, Nr.8

2 **Ich kann sagen, was in der Vergangenheit gerade im Gange war** *(past progressive)*.
• Complete the sentences with the right form of the verbs: past progressive or simple past.

1 I _____ *(make)* dinner when she _____ *(arrived)*.

2 At 8pm last night I _____ *(play)* computer games.

3 When I _____ *(come)* home after school, my brother _____ *(sleep)*.

4 The first time I _____ *(see)* you, you _____ *(wear)* a grey jacket.

WB → S.8–9, Nr.9–12

3 **Ich kann mich beim Arzt verständigen.**
• Complete the sentences with the right words from the box.
You don't need all the words.

| headache • rest • mouth • temperature • hurts • do • tired • flu • sore |

1 My arm _____.

2 I have the _____.

3 What should I _____?

4 Open your _____.

5 I have a _____.

6 My throat is very _____.

7 I feel very _____.

8 You should _____.

WB → S.11, Nr.15–16

Kia ora from New Zealand

1 **Action sports in New Zealand**

🎧 **a** Ariki from New Zealand is talking about some adventure sports.
5   There is one mistake in each sentence below. Listen and correct the information.

---

1 **Rafting** is a great way to enjoy the amazing ~~weather~~ in New Zealand.   *countryside*

The world's highest waterfall for commercial rafting is on New Zealand's

South Island.   _____

The waterfall is 17 metres high.   _____

In Whakarewarewa village you can learn about the music of the Māori people.   _____

---

2 In **heli skiing**, a helicopter takes you to an island where there's snow.   _____

---

3 You can do a **bungee jump** in Auckland's harbour from a famous ship.   _____

NZ's highest bungee is 113 metres.   _____

---

4 Try **zorbing** – you go down a hill in a very big rubber ball!   _____

In 'water zorbing', there's up to 60 litres of water outside the ball.   _____

---

b Find a photo for each sport (1–4 above).
There's one extra photo.

1 _____   2 _____   3 _____   4 _____

SB → *p.27*

2 **MEDIATION** **A great country to visit!**

Nina from New Zealand comes to your school. Your friend Harun wants to ask her some questions about New Zealand, but he doesn't speak good English. Mediate for them.

Harun: Die Landschaft ist unglaublich, oder?

You: _____

Nina: Yes, there are awesome mountains, lakes and geysers.

You: _____

Harun: Mein Vater sagt, in Neuseeland werden viele Filme gedreht. Stimmt das?

You: _____

Nina: Yes, it's surprising how many films were made there.

You: _____

Harun: Ich möchte eine Führung machen. Ich lerne gern Menschen kennen, die dort wohnen.

You: _____

Nina: Come to New Zealand! You can stay at our organic farm.

You: _____

_____

Harun: Vielen Dank! Das ist sehr nett.

You: _____

Nina: You're welcome!

You: _____

SB → p.29

3 **Say NO to discrimination!**

a Students at a school did a project about discrimination. Look at the posters they made. Listen and fill in the missing words.

> **TIP**
>
> Get ready! Read the posters before you listen.

1 SAY NO TO DISCRIMINATION!

Our hearts are all the same

_____

2 SAY NO TO DISCRIMINATION!

A good life is for

_____

3 SAY NO TO DISCRIMINATION!

We all smile in the same

_____ ☺

4 SAY NO TO DISCRIMINATION!

Men, women, rich, poor –

_____ everyone!

5 SAY NO TO DISCRIMINATION!

It's what is on the

_____ that matters.

6 SAY NO TO DISCRIMINATION!

Let's not just say it – let's

_____ it.

7 SAY NO TO DISCRIMINATION!

I say NO to racism!

_____ it now!

8 SAY NO TO DISCRIMINATION!

Try to understand other

people's _____

9 SAY NO TO DISCRIMINATION!

Make a better world where

everyone is _____

b Which three posters do you like best, and why? (Is it funny / clever / true? Do you agree with it?)

I like poster number   because _____

I also like _____

_____

c **MEDIATION** ☉ Choose one poster. ⬤ Choose three posters.
Explain the poster(s) in German to a friend.

_____

_____

_____

d Listen again and repeat the sentences. Use the same intonation[1].

SB → p.31

[1] intonation Betonung

4 Arthur Wharton, footballing legend

1 It's terrible that some people shout racist names at black footballers. But racism isn't a new problem in football. When did the world see its *first* black professional footballer? No, not in the 1980s, or the 1950s... Arthur Wharton, from West

5 Africa, became a professional player in 1889!

Arthur was born in 1865. He went to England in 1882 to study, but he preferred sport. He was good at athletics, cycling and cricket. But football became his sporting career. Wharton played for many football clubs in the north of

10 England from 1886 until 1902. He was a great player.

Arthur faced racism, but he fought back and was a proud man. He was never picked to play for England, although many people thought he was good enough. Was this racism?

Wharton also suffered from class discrimination. His mother

15 was royalty in Africa, but being a footballer made Wharton a lower social class so he couldn't get a job as a government official. After his football career, Warton went to work in a mine. It was hard physical work. He died a poor man in 1930.

But Arthur Wharton is not forgotten! He's remembered as a footballing hero and a black hero.

a Read the article. Write the years.

1 Arthur Wharton was born in Africa in _____ and he came to England in _____.

2 Arthur became a professional footballer in _____.

3 He played for clubs in the North of England from _____ – _____.

4 Arthur Wharton died in _____.

b Tick (✓) the meanings that are right in this text.

1 class [ ] Schulklasse [ ] Stunde [ ] Klasse, Gesellschaftsschicht
[ ] einordnen

2 royalty [ ] Tantieme [ ] Mitglieder des Königshauses

3 official [ ] offiziell [ ] dienstlich [ ] amtlich [ ] Beamte/Beamtin

4 mine [ ] Bergwerk [ ] Mine (Sprengkörper) [ ] meiner/meine/mein(e)s
[ ] graben

c 👥 <mark>Highlight</mark> three positive things and <u>underline</u> three negative things in the text.
Check with a partner.

SB → p.31

5 **A surprise for Sameena**

Complete the text with words from the box. You don't need all the words.

> body • curious • depression • embarrassed • fall out • flat • folder • joins • mix • money • notices

Sameena likes the _____ of students in her class. They sometimes _____ with each

other, but usually they get on well. They often meet in town, but Alison never _____ them.

When they ask her to go bowling with them even her _____ language says 'no'.

Then one day, Sameena takes Alison's art _____ to her house, and gets a surprise. Alison

doesn't live in a big house, but in a small _____. Alison's family has problems: her mum has

_____ and they don't have much _____. Alison feels _____

when Sameena sees how she lives, but she tells Sameena her story. SB → p.34

6 **Words in the story**

Find the <u>opposites</u> of these words and phrases in the story (schoolbook pages 32–33).

1 weaknesses – *(line 1–6)* _____   **2** fall out – *(line 1–6)* _____

3 proud of – *(line 21–28)* _____   **4** under – *(line 36–41)* _____

5 slow – *(line 38–41)* _____   **6** tidy – *(line 79–84)* _____

SB → p.34

7 **What do you think?**

a 📝 What should Sameena and Alison do?
Write your opinion in your exercise book:

> **TIP**
> You can add your own ideas if you wish.

Ideas:
I think Sameena *should / shouldn't* tell other students
about Alison, because it's better if other people
understand / know nothing.
Other students *will / won't* laugh at her.
Alison *should / shouldn't* make friends with other
students.
She'll be *embarrassed / ashamed / happier*.
She'll have more *friends / fun / problems*.
It'll be *easier / more difficult* to be alone.

b 👥 Talk to a partner. Do you agree?

SB → p.34

FOCUS

If-sentences

• Mit if-Sätzen sagst du, was unter bestimmten Bedingungen passieren wird.

    if + simple present + will/'ll oder won't   *If Tim has enough money, he'll go to the cinema*

oder will/'ll oder won't + if + simple present   *Tim will go to the cinema if he has enough money*

---

8 **A trip to New Zealand**

Elise lives in Australia. She's thinking of going to New Zealand in the summer to celebrate her 18th birthday. Complete each sentence with the will-future.

1 If Elise goes to New Zealand, she_____ (have) a great time.

2 And if she works on a farm, the trip _____ (not cost) so much.

3 If it isn't too expensive, she_____(travel) around the country.

4 But if she doesn't have enough money, she _____ (not go) far…

5 …though if Elise takes a tent, the holiday _____ (be) cheaper.

6 If a friend goes with her, they_____ (do) things together.

7 And if they aren't too scared, they_____ (try) bungee jumping!

8 If they really enjoy themselves, they _____ (not want) to come home! SB → p.36

9 ● **Your birthday**

What do you think you'll do for *your* next birthday? Write some ideas.

Ideas:
have … party picnic birthday cake …
go to … beach cinema …
invite … friends Grandma …
go …   bowling swimming …
get …   presents cards …

1 If the weather is good, … _____

2 If I have enough money, … _____

3 If my birthday is on a school day, … _____

4 If my friends can come, … _____

5 If I'm lucky, … _____ SB → p.36

FOCUS

More *If*-sentences

- Der Hauptsatz kann statt will auch can oder einen Imperativ (Befehl) enthalten:

  if + simple present + can   *If you need extra money, you can help more at home*

  if + simple present + imperative   *If you want to find a job, look on the internet*

- Bei allgemein gültigen Wahrheiten steht sowohl im *if*-Satz als auch im Hauptsatz das simple present.

  if + simple present + simple present   *If you work on a farm, you work hard but it's fun*

---

10 **Being a volunteer**

Match the beginnings 1–5 with the right endings a–e. Draw lines.

1 If you're a volunteer,	**a)** apply to help at a nursing home.
2 If you look online,	**b)** you can find lots of ideas for volunteering.
3 For example, if you like animals,	**c)** you don't get paid but it's good experience.
4 If you want to work with older people,	**d)** you can ask to visit it first to have a chat.
5 If you phone the home,	**e)** it's fun to walk dogs for a dogs' home.

SB → p.36

FOCUS

The *going to*-future

- Verwende das going to-future, um über Absichten zu sprechen.

  be (am, are, is) + going to + action verb   Tomorrow we're going to have a picnic.

---

11 **Making money for charity**

Logan and his friends want to make money for charity. What are they going to do? Write the sentences.

1 What / you / do, Logan? _____

_____

2 I / make lots of cakes. _____

3 Then I / sell them. _____

4 Mia and her sister / wash their mum's car. _____

_____

SB → p.37

12 **Describing people**

a Choose the correct adjective from the box. There is one extra.

1 I like to work alone. I don't need help from other people. _____

2 I always have everything I need for lessons – books, extra pens, etc. _____

3 I *always* go to football practice. If I say I'll be there, I *will* be there. _____

4 I speak French very well. When I go to Paris, I'll be OK. _____

5 If there's a new kid in the class, I always go and introduce myself. _____

b Write four sentences about yourself. Use adjectives from the box in a).
I'm very … / quite … / usually … / often … / never …

_____

_____

_____

_____

SB → p.38

13 **Word groups**

Write a name for these groups. Then write more examples.

1 • happy, bored, nervous – They're all *feelings* _____

ashamed, … _____

2 • wardrobe, clock, clothes – They're all *things you can find in* _____

_____

3 • bank, theatre, post office – They're all _____

_____

4 • farmer, hairdresser, shop assistant – They're all _____

_____

SB → p.38

14 READING **Embarrassing or good?**

a Skim through the stories quickly. Does each person talk about an embarrassing thing or a good thing on their first day at work?

	embarrassing	good
Kaia N	☐	☐
Angel R	☐	☐
Ashley M	☐	☐

	embarrassing	good
Frank McL	☐	☐
Luke W	☐	☐

This week: **My first day at work**

Readers' true stories!

My job interview was with the assistant manager, because the manager was away. I met all the people, and they were very friendly.
On my first morning, a young woman arrived at the same time as me. I said "Is it your first day, too? Don't be nervous, they're very nice here." The woman said "No, it isn't my first day. I'm the manager!" I just wanted to die!

Kaia N

When I arrived at work on my first day, the company had won a prize! Everyone was happy. We all drank champagne, and the boss took us to a restaurant. What a great way to start!

Angel R

I started an apprenticeship as a painter and decorator. My boss told me to go to the shop and buy blue and red striped paint[1]. I was so young and nervous, I just did what he said. But when everyone in the shop laughed at me, I suddenly saw the joke – of course striped paint doesn't exist! I felt so stupid.

Ashley M

Forty years ago, on my first morning at work, a beautiful girl smiled at me in the lift. We started to chat. One year later, we were married! Now we have six grandchildren.

Frank McL

On my first morning at work, I wore new trousers and a jacket, and I felt very grown-up[2] and confident. But when I sat down at my desk, the chair broke and I fell onto the floor, with my legs in the air! I wasn't hurt, but I had to walk around all day with a huge hole[3] in the back of my trousers!

Luke W

[1] striped paint gestreifte Wandfarbe   [2] grown up erwachsen   [3] hole Loch

b Look at the stories again. Write the name of the person.

TIP

The questions use *different* words from the text.

1 Which person's boss played a trick on her? _____

2 Which person's office celebrated something? _____

3 Who said something embarrassing to the boss? _____

4 Who had a small accident? _____

5 Who met his future wife? _____

SB → p.39

🎧 **15** **LISTENING** **Talking about jobs**
7
Two young people go back to their old school to talk about their jobs.
Listen and tick the right answers.

1 Ruby …

a ☐ is a teacher.

b ☐ is a football player.

c ☐ is a fitness trainer.

d ☐ is a sports manager.

2 She works in …

a ☐ a gym in the city.

b ☐ a health club in the city.

c ☐ a health club in the country.

d ☐ a gym in the country.

3 For Ruby the best thing about the job is …

a ☐ the hours.

b ☐ helping people to get fit.

c ☐ the pay.

d ☐ that she can use the equipment for free.

4 Josh …

a ☐ is a security guard.

b ☐ is a hairdresser.

c ☐ is training to be a hairdresser.

d ☐ is a supermarket cashier.

5 He likes it because …

a ☐ the pay is good.

b ☐ it's easy.

c ☐ he's very good at it.

d ☐ his colleagues are nice.

6 For Josh the best thing about the job is that …

a ☐ it's about fashion.

b ☐ he makes customers feel good.

c ☐ he meets lots of people.

d ☐ he always has a good day.

SB → p.39

16 **Applying for a job**

You're applying for a summer job in a British supermarket. Fill in this application form.
Fill in the parts that are relevant to you.

> **TIP**
>
> Read the form carefully, including the headings. Make sure you know what information they want!

Personal Details

Title (Mr, Mrs, Ms etc.) _____   Address _____

First Name(s) _____   _____

Last Name _____   _____

Mobile No. _____   Email _____

Are you over 18? ☐ Yes ☐ No   If no, give your date of birth _____

What kind of job are you looking for?   1) ☐ Long-term   ☐ Summer only

2) ☐ Full-time   ☐ Part-time

When could you start? _____

Education and Qualifications

Name of school _____

Exams / Main Subjects _____

_____

College / University _____

Qualification(s) / Main Subjects _____

_____

Other Qualification(s) _____

_____

> Give any qualifications that show your skills,
> e.g. First aid certificate / Judo black belt.

> Write about what you had to do in any part-time job or work experience. E.g. *I was a waitress in a cafe on Saturdays. I had to be polite and helpful to customers and stay calm when it was busy.*

Employment History / Work Experience

1) Where / what / skills _____

_____

_____

2) Where / what / skills _____

_____

_____

More about you

Tell us about your strengths, skills and qualities, and why you would be suitable for a job in our supermarket.

_____

_____

_____

_____

_____

_____

_____

_____

_____

_____

_____

> Think about general things, e.g. being punctual and hard-working...
> ... and also about working in a supermarket, e. g. friendly, helpful, like working with people / helping customers.
> Answer in sentences.

 → p.40

Das kann ich auf Englisch!

Hier kannst du überprüfen, ob und wie gut du alles verstanden hast. Finde auch heraus, wo du dich noch verbessern kannst. Was kannst du schon sehr gut 🟢 oder recht gut 🟡? Was musst du noch üben 🔴? Male die Ampellichter entsprechend aus.

Unit 2

1 **Ich kann sagen, was unter bestimmten Bedingungen geschieht.**
- Complete the sentences with ideas of your own.

1 If my mum gives me 10 Euro, I'll _____ .

2 If I have time on Saturday, _____ .

3 If I'm sick tomorrow, _____ .

4 I'll be very tired if _____ .

5 My English teacher won't be very happy if _____ .

WB → S.19–20, Nr.8–11

2 **Ich kann über Stärken und Schwächen schreiben.**
- Write sentences about strengths and weaknesses.

1 Write a sentence about your positive characteristics: I'm _____

_____ .

2 Write a sentence about your negative characteristics: I'm _____

_____ .

3 What's your best friend like? Describe his / her character.

_____

_____

WB → S.21, Nr.12

3 **Ich kann mich um einen Job bewerben.**
- Match the English words from an application form with their German meaning.

1	first name	**a**	Vollzeitstelle
2	last name	**b**	Handynummer
3	date of birth	**c**	Berufserfahrung
4	mobile number	**d**	Geburtsdatum
5	full time job	**e**	Vorname
6	part-time job	**f**	Teilzeitstelle
7	work experience	**g**	Nachname

WB → S.24–25, Nr.16

Sawubona from South Africa

1 Facts about South Africa

Complete the crossword with words from pages 42–43 in your school book.

Across →

1 The *Big Five* are South Africa's most famous and most **d**... animals.

2 Apartheid was a terrible racist **s**...

4 Under apartheid, black people weren't allowed to **v**....

7 One of the *Big Five*, the **l**..., is often called 'king of the animals'.

8 In some parts of South Africa, people don't have **c**... water.

9 **l**... is still a problem in South Africa – life is often worse for black people than for white.

Down ↓

1 South Africa has **d**... mountains.

3 Zulu is the most widely **s**... language.

5 The country has deserts and a long **c**....

6 English is important, although **f**... than 10 % of people speak it as a first language.

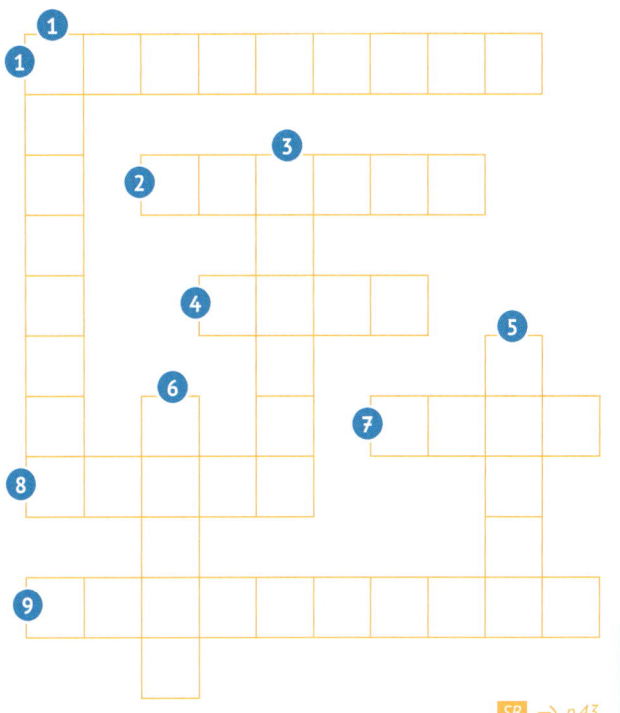

SB → p.43

2 More facts about South Africa

🎧 8

Listen to more information. Circle the right words.

1 South Africa already had many indigenous languages and peoples / cultures / songs.

2 Then people from Holland came and colonized the area in the 15th / 16th / 17th century. They brought slaves / animals / fruit from East Africa and Asia.

3 British colonialists came to South Africa 100 / 200 / 300 years later.

4 After apartheid / a war[1] / a big storm, people called South Africa *the Rainbow[2] Nation*.

5 They hoped it would be a free / rich / multicultural nation where people would live happily together.

6 Tourists love South Africa. The best time to visit is in their summer / winter / spring.

7 That's between March / April / May and August.

8 It is also well-known for its exports of fruit, wine, diamonds and gold / meat / coffee.

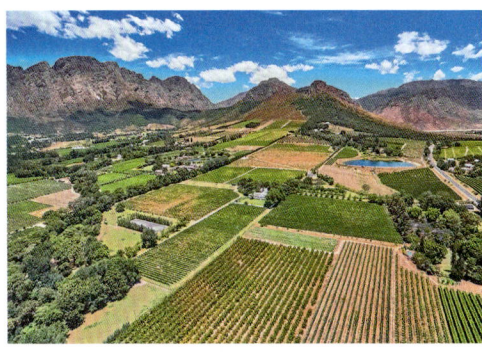

SB → p.43

[1]war Krieg   [2]rainbow Regenbogen

3 **Activities in South Africa**

a   Make sentences about what you can do in different places in South Africa.
Write in your exercise book.

In Kruger National Park			penguins.
In Cape Town		see	local people.
On Boulders Beach	you can	go	a drink in a café with a view of Table Mountain.
On Robben Island		go to	whale watching.
In some townships		meet	the prison where Nelson Mandela spent 18 years.
In Hermanus			on safari.

b   Ask your partner questions.

Do you like
... music?   Yes, I do.
... adventures?   Yes, a bit.
... animals?   Yes, a lot.
... scary things?   No, not really.
... just chilling?   No, not at all.
... finding out about people?   It's OK. / They're OK.

Do you like adventures?

Yes, a lot!

c   Suggest three activities for your partner in South Africa.

I think you should...
It would be... amazing / exciting / fun / interesting / awesome.

SB → p.45

4 **Information on the internet**
Find information about
a   a trip to Robben Island or
b   a whale watching trip on the internet.
Find out the *price, how long it takes and the starting time.*
Write the information in sentences in English.

TIP

South African money
is the *rand.* Find out:
100 rand = _____ euros.

SB → p.45

🎧 **5** **A safari in South Africa**
Luke is talking about the safari he went on in South Africa last year.

a PART A: Tick (✓) the right answers.

1 Luke went on safari with …

a ☐ his mum

b ☐ his aunt

c ☐ his mum and his dad

d ☐ his mum and his aunt.

2 They stayed in …

a ☐ a hotel **b** ☐ a B&B **c** ☐ a tent **d** ☐ a youth hostel.

3 Luke was surprised because …

a ☐ it was small **b** ☐ it wasn't comfortable **c** ☐ it had a bathroom **d** ☐ it was dark.

4 The next morning, they got up at …

a ☐ 4.30 am **b** ☐ 5 am **c** ☐ 5.30 am **d** ☐ 6 am.

5 When they started their morning safari, it was …

a ☐ cold **b** ☐ hot and sunny **c** ☐ hot and dark **d** ☐ rainy.

b PART B: What did the jeep look like? Tick the right picture.

a ☐   b ☐

c PART C True or false?

		True	False
1	They had picnics inside the jeep.	☐	☐
2	They didn't see any lions.	☐	☐
3	You can sometimes find leopards in trees.	☐	☐
4	Elephants don't like lions.	☐	☐
5	Luke saw all the *Big Five* animals.	☐	☐

SB → p.45

6 Young South Africans

Complete the text with words from the box.
You don't need all the words.

> crime • experience • fields • issues •
> products • study • suffer • support •
> unemployed • vlog

Apartheid ended many years ago, but there

are still many *issues*_____ for young

South Africans today. Life in the poor areas is hard, and women _____ most. For example,

sanitary _____ are too expensive. There is still a lot of _____. More than half of

young South Africans are _____ and it's hard to get work _____. Lots

of young people love football, but there aren't enough football _____ where they can play.

But good things are happening too. Many people _____ projects which help young people

who live in poor villages.

SB → p.47

7 Life for young people in Germany

a Read what one person thinks. Draw lines between the beginnings and the endings.

1 There's a lot of stress because you have to...

2 If you don't have much money, ...

3 Some difficult areas have a lot of ...

4 Where I live there are enough ...

5 Influencers tell you to buy things, but ...

6 Most young people have ...

7 We're lucky because we ...

a sports clubs / things for young people.

b follow fashion / be cool / look good /
post on social media.

c enough food / a home / friends.

d crime / drugs / unemployment.

e have lots of free time / have good
schools / there's no war.[1]

f life is quite hard / you can't do
the things you want to.

g you don't have to!

b 👥 What do *you* think about life for young people today? Discuss with a partner.

> One thing that is hard is that ...   What's more, ...   I also think that ...   I agree. / I disagree.
> But on the other hand, ...   It's also true that ...   All in all, I think that ...

SB → p.47

[1] war Krieg

8 Words from the text

a   Read the sentences and find the words in the text in your schoolbook (pages 48–49).

1 It's a place where people sometimes go to study.   *(part A)* _____

2 You can go to hospital in this.   *(part B)* _____

3 It's the opposite of violent.   *(part B)* _____

4 You put clothes in this.   *(part D)* _____

5 You use this for doing yoga.   *(part D)* _____

6 You carry water in this.   *(part D)* _____

b   Describe these things. Use sentences 1–6 above, but change the green words.

1 **cinema**   *It's a place* _____

2 **school bus**   *You can* _____

3 **majority**   _____

4 **garage**   _____

5 **ruler**   _____

6 **school bag**   _____

SB → p.50

9 How to protest

How can you protest? Put the verbs in the sentences.

1 _____ a social media page.

2 _____ a petition .

3 _____ emails.

4 _____ protest songs.

5 _____ on a demonstration.

| go |
| like |
| send |
| sign |
| sing |

You can listen to anti-apartheid protest songs on the internet, e.g. **Free Nelson Mandela** (The Specials), **Bring Him Back Home** (Hugh Masekela), **Never Again** (Prophets of Da City)
Idea: Choose a song you like. Find the song text online. You can also copy the text into a translation[1] app.

SB → p.50

---

[1]translation Übersetzung

FOCUS

Word order

- In Haupt- und Nebensätzen ist die Wortstellung im Englischen: **Subjekt** – Verb – Objekt (S-V-O).
  Last night I saw a film.   *I liked the film because it was funny.*

- Ortsangaben folgen nach dem Verb und Objekt.
  Zeitangaben stehen ganz am Anfang oder ganz am Ende.
  I went to the cinema at 8 o'clock.

---

10 **The Miss World Competition**

a Lerato's mum is talking about her role models.
There are two spaces in each sentence. Put the verb in the right space.

1 Jennifer Hosten is my role model because she _____ the first black *Miss World* _____ . *(was)*

2 I also admire Pearl Jensen from South Africa, because she _____ second _____ . *(came)*

3 At that time in South Africa _____ there _____ the apartheid system. *(was)*

4 In 1970 _____ we _____ two *Miss South Africas*: a black woman and a white woman. *(had)*

5 The two women were friendly when they _____ interviews together _____ . *(did)*

6 But they weren't really *friends* because apartheid _____ them unequal _____ . *(made)*

The Miss World Competition,
November 11th, 1970, London

From left to right:
Miss Israel (Irith Lavi) (3rd)
Miss South Africa (Jillian Jessup) (5th)
Miss Grenada / Miss World (Jennifer Hosten) (1st)
Miss Africa South (Pearl Jensen) (2nd)
Miss Sweden (Marjorie Johansson) (4th)

b Put the words in the right order.

1 But my biggest role models are the women who protested during the competition.

They said that _____ . | sexist / it / was |

2 In 2020 _____ . | a film about it / made / they |

3 I was happy that _____ .

| played / the main character / Keira Knightley |

4 That's because _____ . | she / my favourite actor / is | 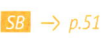 → *p.51*

11 A famous child
Write the phrases from the boxes in the right order.

The Taung Child

1 | in 1924 • near the town of Taung | A very famous child from South Africa is the

"Taung Child". It was found _____

2 | in the ground • one day | Workers found an old skull[1] _____

3 | in the house • a few days later | The company boss gave it to his son, and a friend saw the skull

_____

4 | at that time • at the university | She sent it to Professor Dart, an expert who was working

_____

5 | in a scientific magazine • only forty days later | He said it was a child, who came from a species[2]

before modern people. He called the species *Australopithecus africanus*. He put an article

_____

6 | 2.5 million years ago • near Taung | Amazingly, scientists think that the child died

_____ !

SB → *p.52*

12 MEDIATION At the museum
Lerato and her friend are at the Origins Centre museum at Wits University. They meet a German boy who is too shy to speak English. Lerato mediates for him. Complete her sentences.

1 | Das ist ein großartiges Museum! Ich kam gestern hierher und ich bin heute wiedergekommen.

1 *This is* _____

_____

2 | Ich bin aufgeregt, weil Professor Dart vor 100 Jahren an dieser Universität von dem Taung-Kind berichtet hat.

2 *I'm excited because Professor Dart wrote*

about _____

_____

3 | Ich habe das Neandertal-Museum in der Nähe von Düsseldorf letzten Monat besucht. Es war toll! Ich liebe Geschichte wirklich.

3 *I visited the Neanderthal Museum*

_____

_____

SB → *p.52*

[1] skull Schädel   [2] species (Menschen-)Art

13 Springboks – the animals
Read the text about springboks and (circle) the correct words.

The springbok has been the national animal of South Africa since / for / by many years. It is a kind of / from / for antelope that lives in southern and south-western Africa. This beautiful animal is about a metre tall and it has horns[1] which / who / where are 35 – 50 cm long.

The springbok eats grass and plants.

Amazed / Amazing / Amazingly , it can live for years without water – it doesn't has / having / have to drink because it gets enough water in its food!

Sometimes, the springbok does a funny thing called "pronking": it jumps / jump / jumped high into the air (up to 2 m!), with all four legs at the same time. Experts don't really now / know / no why it does this! It can also run very fast – up to 88 km per hour. That's a lot faster as / than / from a leopard!

SB → p.53

14 Springboks – the sports team
Read the text. Change the words to make them fit the sentence.

My uncle Johann has *(live)* _____ in Johannesburg since 2015. We often go to stay with him,

and he *(visit)* _____ us in Durban. He's a PE teacher, and he *(teach)* _____ me to

play rugby when I was little. I'm really *(interest)* _____ in sport, and I *(special)*

_____ like rugby. We love watching the Springboks – that's what everyone calls our

national rugby team. Once, I met some *(play)* _____ from the team after the match.

I felt a bit *(embarrass)* _____, but really happy! It was the *(good)* _____ day

of my life!

SB → p.53

---

[1] horns Hörner

🎧 **15** **LISTENING** **At the police station 1**
10

a A man has come to the police station. Complete the police form. Write notes.

North Street Police Station – Lost items form	
What has been lost?	
Where was it lost?	
When was it lost?	
Description:	
What is in it?	

b What happens at the end?

They give him _____

He must phone his _____ to tell them about his _____

SB → p.56

16 **SPEAKING** **At the police station 2**

a • Partner A goes into a police station to say that he/she has lost something.
Partner B is the police officer.
Imagine the conversation, and how it ends.
• Then swap roles.

> Can I help you?
> Where / when did you lose it?
> Can you describe your ...?
> What make is the ...?
> What is its value?
> What's in it?

Partner A:	Partner B:

TIP

You can invent the details that aren't in the pictures.

b 📝 Write one of the dialogues in your exercise book.

SB → p.56

17 WRITING 📝 **A picture story**

Look at the pictures and write a story in English in your exercise book. Write at least 80 words.

> **TIPP**
>
> Schreibe mindestens 100 Wörter.
> Achte auf eine ansprechende äußere Form.

> **TIPP**
>
> Wenn in der Aufgabenstellung angegeben ist, dass du mindestens 80 Wörter schreiben sollst, darfst du nicht weniger schreiben.
> Um sicherzugehen, dass du wirklich genug schreibst, hier eine Hilfe: das sind durchschnittlich 13 Wörter pro Bild.
> Du kannst hinzufügen, was die Leute sagen, z.B. "...," she said   "...," he answered.

Start like this:

The lost car keys

On Monday morning, Mrs Green was in a panic because...

where – car key?

looked for – couldn't find

clock – late

bike – too big

ran – bus stop – too late

surprise – toy car[1]

SB → p.57

---

[1] toy car Spielzeugauto

Das kann ich auf Englisch!

Hier kannst du überprüfen, ob und wie gut du alles verstanden hast. Finde auch heraus, wo du dich noch verbessern kannst. Was kannst du schon sehr gut ● oder recht gut ●? Was musst du noch üben ●? Male die Ampellichter entsprechend aus.

Unit 3

1 **Ich kenne Aspekte der Geschichte Südafrikas.**
- Complete the sentences with the correct word.

1 Black people weren't allowed to _____ under the apartheid system.

2 People from _____ colonized South Africa in the 16th century.

3 The island where Nelson Mandela spent 18 years in prison is called _____.

WB → *S. 27, Nr. 2*

2 **Ich kann sprachliche Regelmäßigkeiten erkennen** *(Wortstellung).*
- Complete the sentences by putting the words in brackets in the right order.

1 Elephants can't see very well _____.
> are • their eyes • because • so small

2 They can hear other elephants _____.
> away • more than 10 km • which • are

3 Female[1] elephants start having babies _____.
> they • about 14 years old • are • when

WB → *S. 32, Nr. 10*

3 **Ich kann den Verlust eines Gegenstands bei der Polizei anzeigen.**
- Complete the dialogue with the questions in the box. There is one extra.

> Where did you lose it? • Can I help you? •
> When did you lose it? • Can you describe it, please?

Police officer: Good morning. _____

Girl: Yes, please. I've lost my purse.

Police officer: _____

Girl: Yesterday afternoon, when I was coming home from school.

Police officer: _____

WB → *S. 36, Nr. 16–17*

Girl: I think I left it on the bus.

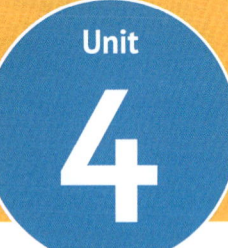
Namaste from India

🎧 **1** **A tour around India**
11
a Listen to tourist information about different parts of India. For each part, tick (✓) all the things that the people talk about.

Things they talk about:	North India	West India	Northeast & East India	South India
hills/mountains				
beaches				
special buildings (e.g. palaces/temples/forts)				
shopping/eating				
animals				
desert				
nightlife				

the Golden Temple of Amritsar

growing tea in Darjeeling

b Which part(s) of India would you most like to visit, and why?

I'd like to visit ... because ...

c 👥 Compare with a partner and discuss your answers.

SB → p.59

2 **Indian history**

a Complete the puzzle with words from the texts on page 60 of your schoolbook.

1 In the 18th century, many Indians had no money – they lived in extreme ... .

2 In the 16th century, ships took ... products around the world.

3 Indians invented the ... (0) – important for maths and technology.

4 Gandhi was an important ... in India's campaign for independence.

5 In the 5th century, the Indian astronomer, Aryabhata, wrote that the earth was ... .

6 In 1947, part of western India became ... .

7 The game of ... was invented in India hundreds of years ago.

8 Indian ... still study the earth and the planets today.

b Write the answer to question 9 (down ↓):

9 What is the name of the oldest city in India that people still live in today? _____

c ● ℚ Check your answer to b). Then find out more information about this city on the internet:

1 What river is it on? _____

2 How old is it? _____

3 How many temples does it have? about _____ !

SB → p.61

3 **Two national heroes**

You've learned about Mahatma Gandhi (schoolbook page 61) and Nelson Mandela (schoolbook page 48). Are these sentences true for one of these men or both? Tick (✓) the right boxes.

	Gandhi	Mandela
1 He worked as a lawyer.		
2 He protested against laws that were unfair.		
3 He campaigned for independence for his country.		
4 He became president of his country.		
5 He was killed.		

SB → p.61

4 **The love story of the Taj Mahal**

Listen to this radio programme about the Taj Mahal. Tick (✓) the right answers.

1 The Taj Mahal is in the ...

  a ☐ north   **b** ☐ south

  c ☐ east   **d** ☐ west   ... of India.

2 It is a ...   **a** ☐ mosque   **b** ☐ temple

             c ☐ palace   **d** ☐ mausoleum[1].

3 The prince married the beautiful girl, Arjumand, ...

  a ☐ 5   **b** ☐ 7

  c ☐ 12   **d** ☐ 16   ... years after they met.

4 She was his ...   **a** ☐ first   **b** ☐ second   **c** ☐ third   **d** ☐ only   ... wife.

5 Shah Jahan called his wife Mumtaz Mahal, which means ...

  a ☐ the beautiful one.

  b ☐ the favourite one.

  c ☐ the chosen one of the palace.

  d ☐ the queen of the palace.

6 Mumtaz Mahal was popular because ...

  a ☐ she helped Shah Jahan.

  b ☐ she gave food and money to the poor.

  c ☐ she was beautiful.

  d ☐ she was clever.

7 Mumtaz Mahal died just after her ...

  a ☐ 11th   **b** ☐ 13th   **c** ☐ 14th   **d** ☐ 16th   child was born.

8 Special stone for the Taj Mahal, white marble[2], was brought by a thousand ...

  a ☐ workers   **b** ☐ slaves   **c** ☐ horses   **d** ☐ elephants

9 Shah Jahan spent his last years ...

  a ☐ in prison   **b** ☐ in the Taj Mahal   **c** ☐ with his son   **d** ☐ with his last wife.

SB → p.63

[1] mausoleum Mausoleum   [2] marble Marmor

5 MEDIATION **A vegetarian curry**

a   Your friend wants to eat more vegetarian food to help the environment. She's found this recipe.
Can you match these German words with the green words in the recipe?

1 Esslöffel _____   5 Kichererbsen _____

2 Kokosnuss _____   6 Pulver _____

3 fein gehackt _____   7 Knoblauch _____

4 Spinat _____

Quick Chickpea Curry
for 4 people

1 onion, chopped
½ red or green chilli, finely chopped
2 cloves of garlic, finely chopped
1 tablespoon garam masala curry powder
1 400g can of chopped tomatoes
2 400g cans of chickpeas
1 400g can of coconut milk
100 g spinach

- Fry the onion in a little oil until it is golden.
- Add the garlic, chilli and garam masala, and fry for one minute.
- Then add the tomatoes, chickpeas (without the water), coconut milk, salt and pepper.
- When everything is hot, cook for 10 minutes. Put in the spinach and cook for two more minutes.
- Serve with rice.

---

b   Make notes in German in your exercise book so your friend can make the curry.   SB → p.63

6 **Climate change**

Change the words in orange. Find words and phrases in the box that mean the same thing. You don't need all the words.

| drones • drought • forest • growing • heatwaves • melts • on the coast • pollution • rise |

India's economy is getting bigger (*growing*_____) fast. But the country has problems. Perhaps

the biggest is climate change. Times of very hot weather (_____) have already killed

thousands of people. Many Indians live next to the sea (_____), and if more ice

turns into water (_____), sea levels will go up (_____), and these people could lose

their homes. Another big danger is not enough water (_____). This is a problem for farms,

factories and people's health. Indians hope that electric cars will help to stop climate change and

dirty air (_____) in their cities.   SB → p.65

7 **Words from the text**

a Find these words in the text *'A mission to the moon'* in your schoolbook on pages 66–67.

1 This is the part of a computer that shows words and pictures. *(lines 1–6)* ☐ ☐ 🟨 ☐ ☐ ☐

2 It means 'without any problems'. *(lines 7–14)* ☐ ☐ ☐ ☐ ☐ ☐ ☐ 🟨

3 You see this in the sky at night. *(lines 7–14)* ☐ ☐ ☐ 🟨

4 This means 'make a lot of progress'. *(lines 15–20)* 🟨 ☐ ☐ ☐ ☐ ☐ ☐

5 This means 'at that time in the past'. *(lines 15–20)* ☐ ☐ ☐ ☐ 🟨 ☐ ☐

6 This is another word for a small wagon. *(lines 25–30)* ☐ 🟨 ☐ ☐

7 This is another word for a country. *(lines 33–37)* ☐ 🟨 ☐ ☐ ☐ ☐

8 A lot of water on the ground, after heavy rain, for example *(lines 50–56)* ☐ ☐ ☐ ☐ ☐ 🟨 ☐

9 When a screen has nothing on it, it's ... *(lines 67–78)* ☐ ☐ ☐ 🟨 ☐

10 To hear nothing from someone/something = to lose ... *(lines 67–78)* ☐ ☐ ☐ ☐ ☐ 🟨 ☐ ☐

11 This is someone who goes into space. *(lines 83–88)* ☐ ☐ ☐ ☐ ☐ ☐ 🟨 ☐ ☐

b The letters in yellow make an anagram of the name of the Indian spacecraft launched in 2019. What is its name? (You can find it in the text.)

 – 2

c *Sanskrit* is a very old Indian language – about 3,500 years old! *Chandra* means 'moon' in Sanskrit, and *yaan* means 'craft' (as in 'spacecraft'). So what could you call the Indian spacecraft in German?

 *SB* → *p.68*

8 📋✍ **Being an astronaut**
What do you think – what's it like to be an astronaut? Write your answer in your exercise book.

Ideas:
I think it's probably (quite / very) ...
but it's also ... exciting / scary / hard / dangerous / ...
You have to ... be very fit / work hard / leave your family / train for a long time / ...
I would / wouldn't like to ... go into space / ...
I give this story ... stars

 *SB* → *p.68*

FOCUS

The simple past and present perfect

- Mit dem present perfect sagst du, dass du etwas schon einmal, manchmal, oft, oder noch nie gemacht hast. Signalwörter: *ever, never, often, up to now, yet, since, for.*
  I've often walked to school, but I haven't cycled.
- Mit dem simple past sagst du, was zu einem bestimmten Zeitpunkt in der Vergangenheit passiert ist. Die Handlung ist vorbei. Signalwörter: bestimmter Tag oder Datum, *yesterday, last week, a year ago.*
  I went to school by bus yesterday, but I didn't see my friend Abhi on the bus.

9 **Our school Environment Club**

The school has a new club to help the environment. This crossword will help you learn some past participles.

TIP

You can find a list of irregular verbs on page 61 in this book.

Across →

3 Our teacher has *(give)* us lots of help to start the club.
5 We've already *(have)* some ideas about planting trees.
6 We haven't *(begin)* work in the organic garden yet.
9 We haven't *(buy)* new equipment – it's all second-hand.
10 Anika has *(find)* information about recycling.

Down ↓

1 We've *(write)* a list of things we want to do.
2 The club hasn't *(meet)* very often up to now.
4 We've *(made)* some money for an environmental group.
7 Since we started, the club has *(grow)* to 35 members.
8 Ali has *(put)* posters up in school about climate change.

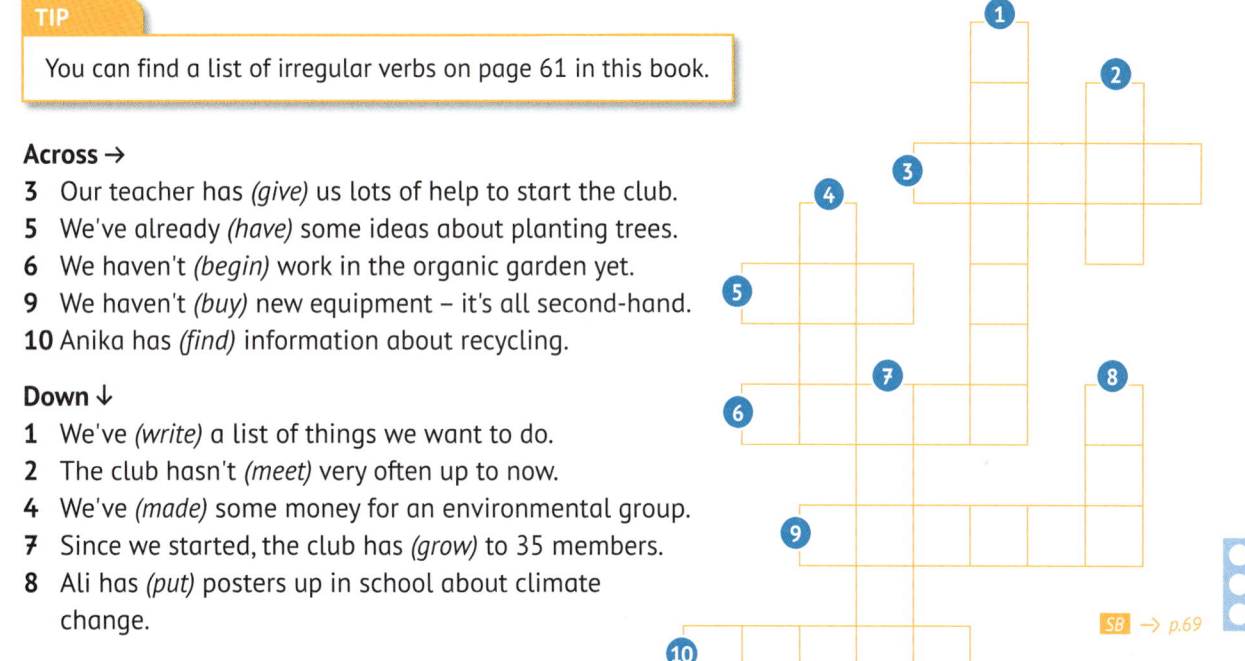

SB → p.69

10 **Two months later ...**

What have the club members done? What haven't they done yet? Use the present perfect.

1 We_____ rubbish out of a local river. *(take)*

2 We_____ trees and vegetables, but we

_____ any vegetables yet. *(plant; not sell)*

3 We _____ chemicals. *(not use)*

4 We_____ two climate change protests. *(join)*

5 But we _____ our website. *(not build)*

6 And we _____ a good logo yet. *(not choose)*

SB → p.69

11 **Tigers in India and around the world**

a Read the article. <u>Underline</u> the signal words and phrases for the present perfect.
Highlight the signal words and phrases for the simple past.

At the start of the 20th century, over 100,000 tigers have lived /
lived in many countries across the world. But since then, the
number of tigers has fallen / fell to a few thousand, and tigers
have gone / went completely from some countries. In 2010,
there have been / were around only 3,200 wild tigers. All those
tigers haven't died / didn't die in the 20th century from natural
causes – people have killed / killed many of them for sport or
because they haven't liked / didn't like having dangerous
animals near their villages. Up to now, we haven't taken /
didn't take enough care of these beautiful animals. People
have hunted / hunted tigers and they have killed / killed too
many.

b (Circle) the right verb form.

SB → *p.70*

12 **Better news about tigers**

a <u>Underline</u> the signal words for the present perfect.
Highlight the signal words and phrases for the simple past.

In 2010, thirteen countries _____ (have) a big meeting in Russia. They _____

(discuss) how to the save the tigers, and different countries and celebrities _____ (give) money.

Since 2010 people _____ (work) hard to

save the tiger and the number has grown (grow) a lot.

In 2019, experts _____ (think) the number was

around 3,900. The number _____

(continue) to rise since then. The first International Tiger Day

_____ (take place) over 10 years ago and _____

_____ (happen) every year since that time.

International
TIGER DAY
let us put an end to their despair

b Write the verbs in the right tense:
present perfect or simple past.

> **TIP**
>
> When you use the *present perfect*,
> check if you need *has* or *have*.

SB → *p.70*

13 Visiting family in Mumbai

Circle the right pronouns in the text.

My brother and I went to stay in Mumbai with we / our / us aunt and uncle and their / them / they four cats.

My uncle took me / I / my and my brother to him / her / his favourite street food seller, where I had the famous Mumbai *vada pav*. It / He / She is a sort of spicy potato sandwich! A friend of my uncle's saw he / him / her and she came over and chatted to we / us / our. She's a singer and gave us tickets for his / her / she next concert! My aunt and uncle are really nice. We're going to stay with they / them / their again in the summer.

 SB → p.70

14 👥 The adjective game

a Can you write adjectives that begin with these letters of the alphabet?
• Work alone first. Then compare with your partner.
• You get one point for each adjective – and an extra point if your partner doesn't have the same word!

> **TIP**
>
> Think of colours; describing a person, a place, a thing, feelings, the weather, etc. E.g. *big, spicy, nervous*

a _____   n _____

b _____   o _____

c _____   p _____

d _____   q _____

e _____   r _____

f _____   s _____

g _____   t _____

h _____   u _____

i _____   w _____

l _____   y _____

m _____

b With your partner, think of a noun to go with each adjective.

an *awesome* song

blue sky

 SB → p.70

🎧 **15** **LISTENING** 🔵 **An accident**
13

Ariv saw an accident this morning. Later he tells a police officer what happened – but he makes some mistakes! Listen to the conversation and circle in the picture the details he gets wrong! The first is done as an example; there are <u>five</u> more.

SB → p.71

16 **SPEAKING** 👥 **Are you a good witness[1]?**

• Look carefully at the accident in Picture A or B for one minute. Then close your book.
• Can you remember the details? Tell your partner what happened.
He/she can ask questions to help you.

What happened?	crashed into skidded
What did ... look like?	fell off stopped suddenly
Was ... hurt?	knocked over was bleeding
What time did it happen?	ran across
Did ... have a helmet?	

Partner A

Partner B

SB → p.71

---

[1]witness Zeuge/Zeugin

17 **READING** Deepika Padukone, Bollywood star

a Read the text and put the sections in the right order.

1	2	3	4	5	6
E					

A What are Deepika's plans for the future? More acting and producing? Family? Who knows – but her tens of millions of followers on social media will soon hear her news!

B Since she started, Deepika has been in over thirty films of all kinds. Her films have been very successful and have made a lot of money. And Deepika has also started to produce films too.

C Deepika Padukone was born in Copenhagen, Denmark. The family moved to Bangalore, India, when Deepika was a baby. As a child, Deepika played badminton at national level and was very good at baseball too. But she was also a child model, and at the age of 16, she decided to stop playing sport and become a fashion model.

D But all these successful films have not always made Deepika happy. In 2014 she got help for depression. A few days before her wedding to actor Ranveer Singh, she wrote about her depression in a magazine and later spoke on television. She hoped that this would help other people. In June 2015 she started the Live, Love, Laugh Foundation, which helps people who have mental health problems and she continues to work hard for this.

E Deepika Padukone is one of the most famous women in India. A top film actor, film producer and fashion icon, Deepika is one of the most popular Indian celebrities.

F After leaving school, Deepika became a full-time model and soon had roles in TV adverts too. She moved to Mumbai, the centre of India's film industry, where she stayed with her aunt. She went to an acting school and soon got a part in her first film, a romantic comedy.

b Answer these questions:

1 How many films has Deepika acted in? _____

2 What sports was Deepika good at? _____

3 When did she give up sport? _____

4 What job does her husband[1] do? _____

5 What problem did Deepika have? _____

6 Who did she live with when she went to Mumbai? _____ SB → p.72

[1] husband Ehemann

Das kann ich auf Englisch!

Hier kannst du überprüfen, ob und wie gut du alles verstanden hast. Finde auch heraus, wo du dich noch verbessern kannst. Was kannst du schon sehr gut ● oder recht gut ●? Was musst du noch üben ●? Male die Ampellichter entsprechend aus.

Unit 4

1 **Ich kann über Umweltschutz sprechen.**
• Match the words with their meaning.

drought	dirty air
forest	an area with lots of trees
heatwave	a time of very hot weather
air-pollution	Ice does this when it gets warm.
melt	a time when there is no rain

WB → S.41, Nr.6

2 **Ich kann sprachliche Regelmäßigkeiten erkennen** *(simple past and present perfect)*.
• Circle the right verb form: simple past or present perfect.

1 I was / have been born in Heidelberg.

2 I was / have been at school for 9 years.

3 My sister left / has left school three years ago.

4 My family came / has come to Munich when I was five years old.

5 I play football. I played / 've played for the same team since 2020.

WB → S.43–44, Nr.9–12

3 **Ich kann von einem Unfall berichten.**
• Look at the picture of an accident and write answers to the questions.

1 What happened? _____

_____

2 Who did they phone? _____

_____

3 Was anybody hurt? _____

_____

WB → S.46, Nr.15–16

1 Declan's birthday

a Listen to a phone conversation between Declan and his Uncle John.
While you listen, tick (✓) the correct answers or complete the sentences.

14

1 For his birthday, Uncle John gave Declan …

a ☐ money.

b ☐ science fiction books.

c ☐ a DVD.

d ☐ a phone.

2 On his birthday, Declan …

a ☐ stayed at home.

b ☐ played tennis.

c ☐ went swimming.

d ☐ went to the beach.

3 In the evening, they …

a ☐ saw a film.

b ☐ watched TV.

c ☐ went to the theatre.

d ☐ went to a concert.

4 The pet Uncle John is going to get is

_____ .

5 He has chosen this pet because it's …

a ☐ cuter.

b ☐ cheaper to buy.

c ☐ cheaper to look after.

d ☐ easier to look after.

6 Uncle John will come to Declan's house at

_____ .

b What was the best birthday present you ever got? Why?

_____

_____

_____

SB → p.97

2 Samira's terrible day

Declan's friend Samira phones Declan and tells him about her terrible day.
There is one mistake in each sentence below. Listen and write the correct information on the line.

1 I had to go to school by bike because my mum's car wouldn't start.

_____

2 It was sunny when I left the house at 8.30.

_____

3 I was texting and I crashed into the back of the car in front of me.

_____

4 I wasn't hurt badly, but my hand is a bit sore and I got a shock.

_____

5 Luckily, my bike is OK – I only got it three weeks ago!

_____

6 I arrived an hour too late for the maths lesson.

_____

SB → p.97

3 A phone message

Samira's dad, Mr Khan, has a voicemail message.
Listen and write the missing information.

1 The message is from: _____

2 Car number: ZH65 _____

3 A problem with: _____

4 What they need to do:

_____

5 The garage opens tomorrow at:

_____

6 The car will be ready:

_____

SB → p.97

1 **A tour with a difference**

Read the text about an interesting tour. Find <u>eight</u> mistakes in the text and write the correct word on the numbered line. Write only <u>one</u> word to correct the mistake.

You've heard of *bus* tours ..., but who is a *Rebus* tour? Well,

1 _____

it's a special tour you can go on at Edinburgh, Scotland's

2 _____

capital city. Detective Inspector John Rebus is the main

character in the crime novels of Scottish writer Ian Rankin.

Rebus works in the city, and the tours taking fans to some of

3 _____

the places in the books. These aren't typical tourist places –

they aren't the most beautiful areas of Edinburgh – but much

4 _____

of them show the dark and secret sides of the city and its

history. You visit places who are found in the novels, and

5 _____

you also learn about Edinburgh's history and some of the

famous people who lives there.

6 _____

A walking tour as this is a great way to get to know this

7 _____

interested city.

8 _____

SB → p.99

2 **Hobbies**

Samira has written an email to her German exchange partner.
Fill each gap with <u>one</u> word that fits the sentence. Do not change the text.

Hi Jonas

In your last email you _____ me if I liked reading. Yes, I _____.

I usually read about two or three books _____ week. My favourite

books are crime novels – I love them because they're so _____. What

_____ of books do you like? I like _____ crime series on TV too.

_____ about you? What are your favourite programmes? _____ there any British

crime programmes on German TV? Have you _____ read any crime novels by British writers?

SB → p.99

3 **Advice from friends**

Declan asks his friends a question on a social media site. Some words are missing from the text. Choose the most appropriate answer (A, B, C or D) for each gap (1-8) in the text. Write your answers in the boxes after the text.

Declan	I'm thinking of getting a tattoo. What do you __1__ ?
Ryan	No, __2__ do it, Declan! In two years' time you might not like it. Think about it for a few months first, then you can decide.
Grace	I think you should __3__ a tattoo – they're really cool.
Jimi	I had a tattoo done three months __4__ . I thought it was great, but when my mum saw it, she __5__ crazy! ☹
Ella	You can't, Declan – you __6__ be 18 for a tattoo in the UK. Sorry – __7__ too young.
Declan	Thanks, guys. It looks like I'll have to wait __8__ I'm 18, and decide then.

1 A thought   B think   C thinks   D thinking

2 A don't   B can't   C won't   D didn't

3 A become   B take   C get   D buy

4 A for   B ago   C before   D away

5 A go   B going   C goes   D went

6 A will   B needn't   C have to   D can

7 A yours   B you're   C you   D your

8 A before   B while   C when   D until

1	2	3	4	5	6	7	8

 SB → p.99

1 **An article in a school magazine**

TIP

Dictionary allowed

Our school exchange

Last October was our first exchange visit to Germany. _(1)_ They all enjoyed this new experience very much. It was clear that our students' German improved during the visit, and they made some very good friends. _(2)_

Then this year in the May half-term holiday, we welcomed our exchange partners from Germany for the first time. They stayed with our students and their families and very much enjoyed their experience of British life. _(3)_

On some of the days, our guests were with their British exchange partners and their families, but on other days, we met up as one big group and did things together. One of the highlights was the trip to Ilfracombe. Everyone enjoyed having fish and chips down at the harbour. _(4)_ The seagulls would have had some too, if we had let them!

In the afternoon, half of the group went to the Aquarium and the other half went on a boat trip and saw lots of sea birds and some seals. _(5)_ Everyone had great fun and bought presents to take home.

We all took lots of great photos during the exchange. _(6)_ We are already discussing a trip to Germany in spring and we hope that our school exchange will go on for many years to come.

Read the text. Six sentences are missing from it. Read sentences A–G and match them with the gaps 1–6. There is <u>one</u> extra sentence.

(1) _____

(2) _____

(3) _____

(4) _____

(5) _____

(6) _____

A Luckily, no-one was sea-sick!

B We are all sure it will.

C It was a typical British seaside lunch.

D So of course they were looking forward to meeting again this year.

E We have put them up on the school website.

F And it was cheaper than a youth hostel.

G None of our students had been to Germany before.

SB → p.101

2 **Saving lives at sea**

TIP

Dictionary allowed

1 The town of Ilfracombe in Devon, south-west England, has had a lifeboat[1] station for nearly 180 years. At the moment, the station has two lifeboats, which are run by the RNLI.

The RNLI (Royal National Lifeboat Institution), a famous organisation in
5 Britain, is a charity that saves lives at sea. The organisation was founded in 1824 and since then it has saved more than 140,000 people's lives and has helped thousands more people to get back to dry land from the sea.

Around the UK and Ireland there are 237 RNLI lifeboat stations, with a total of 346 lifeboats. There are 4,600 lifeboat crew members – and most of them work here on a voluntary basis. Most of them
10 have other jobs. For example, there are teachers, office workers, garage mechanics and university students. When they are called to help, these people must stop what they're doing and go to the lifeboat station as fast as possible, day or night.

The biggest rescue in the RNLI's history was on 17 March 1907 when a huge ship hit rocks off the coast of Cornwall. Fighting through stormy winds and fog, RNLI lifeboats worked for sixteen hours
15 and rescued 456 people, including 70 babies.

These RNLI volunteers are brave people. Their work is dangerous, and they risk their own lives to help other people.

Read the text. Then write the answers to the questions.
Do not write sentences. Write numbers, words or notes only.

1 How long has there been a lifeboat station in Ilfracombe?

_____

2 What does the RNLI do?

_____

3 How many lives has it saved since it began?

_____

4 How many boats does the RLNI have?

_____

5 How much money do most RNLI workers get for rescuing people?

_____

6 Describe the weather on the day of the RNLI's biggest rescue.

_____

SB → p.101

[1] lifeboat Rettungsboot

1 **A part time job**

Luana aus deiner Klasse braucht deine Hilfe. Ihre Schwester möchte Geld als Straßenkünstlerin verdienen. Luanas britischer Brieffreund hat ihr diesen Artikel geschickt.

TIP

Dictionary allowed

Schreibe für Luanas Schwester eine Zusammenfassung des Artikels. Sie interessiert sich besonders für folgende Fragen:

- Welche Musik sollte man singen?
- Welche Uhrzeit ist am besten?
- Hast du sonst noch Tipps?
- Wo sollte man am besten singen?
- Gibt es besondere Regeln bezüglich Straßenmusik?
- Gibt es andere Tätigkeiten, mit denen man auf der Straße Geld verdienen kann?

A great way to earn money

1   A friend of mine gave me some tips for success in busking. A good idea is to sing songs that are popular, that people want to hear. And of course your act should be family-friendly. Finding a good time and place to busk is important, for example, a place where a lot of people come to shop on a Saturday or at lunchtime. Of course, you also have to check the rules about busking in your town,

5   for example, you might need a busking licence.

There are other important tips. For a start, you have to be willing to practise. People won't give you money if you're just not very good – and why should they! And have respect for other people. For example, don't

10   be too loud, or spend hours in front of the same shop.

And there are a few downsides to busking. Make sure you're wearing lots of warm clothes if it's cold outside. Also, some people can be very unkind and make stupid comments about your performance. But don't get stressed by that – don't think about it!

Of course, playing the guitar and singing isn't the only kind of busking – there are other kinds. Do

15   you have circus skills such as juggling or acrobatics? Or maybe dancing or being a 'living statue'. It's a good idea to do something original and be different from other buskers, but the main thing is to be good at what you do. Happy busking!

SB → p.103

2 **A fitness tracker**

Dein Freund möchte einen Fitness Tracker kaufen. Du findest die folgenden Bewertungen im Internet. Lies die Bewertungen durch und trage die wichtigsten Punkte auf Deutsch in die Tabelle ein.

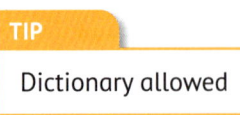

TIP

Dictionary allowed

Geno ★★★★☆ **A great fitness tracker**

I bought this fitness tracker two months ago and I wear it all the time. It does all the things I want it to. I can check how many steps I've done and how many miles I do every day. I can check my heart rate, which is also useful. Another good feature is that it tells you how long you were asleep for and how well you slept. I would definitely recommend this fitness tracker. However, it took me a long time to work out how to use it, because the instructions aren't very good. So if you haven't had a fitness tracker before, get a friend to help you get started.

JD ★★★☆☆ **Good value**

I like this fitness tracker and it has some great features. It has GPS, which is useful. Normally, the battery lasts about 12 days, but if you use the GPS it only lasts four hours, which won't be enough for a lot of people. My favourite thing is that it tells you when you've been sitting for too long! So there's no excuse for being lazy! I go swimming a lot, so that's why I chose this fitness tracker – because it's waterproof so you can wear it while you swim. One problem is that the fitness tracker is difficult to read when it's sunny, which is really annoying. Apart from that, I think it's a good fitness tracker, and a great price.

Was der Fitness Tracker kann:	• Er zählt deine Schritte und die Kilometerzahl, die du gelaufen bist. • Du kannst deinen Herzschlag überprüfen. • _____ • Er hat eine GPS-Funktion. • _____ • _____
Batterie:	• _____ _____ _____
Was ist nicht so gut?	• Die _____ • _____ _____

SB → p.103

1 **Read the conversation. Then write James's birthday invitation. Write all the important information.**

James: Mum, I'm thinking about having a birthday party. What do you think?

Mum: What kind of party? And where? And how many people? You know what happened last time you had a party, don't you?

James: Yes, mum, I said I was sorry. I'd like to invite my friends home – some friends from school and some from the football club. And the neighbours too. Maybe twenty people? We can play computer games and eat pizza.

Mum: If you want twenty friends, you're not having a party here. Who will have to clean it all up afterwards? Me, of course! Why not go to the park or the swimming pool? Or go to the cinema?

James: OK, maybe a pool party would be cool. We can take some food and buy ice creams there. When can I do it? The weekend after my birthday?

Mum: Yes, the Sunday would be best. What date is that? The 14th June.

James: No, mum, that's no good. I have a big dancing competition that day. We should have it on the day before – on the Saturday.

Mum: Yes, OK. In the afternoon? About 2?

James: Yes, in the afternoon, but maybe a bit later. Maybe at half past three?

Mum: OK, if you like. That's fine. And tell your friends to bring some things to eat and drink. I can't make food for 20 people!

James: I'll remind them to bring their swimming costumes and towels too. And some money for ice creams.

Mum: That's OK, James. I'll give you some money for your friends' ice creams. They don't need to bring money. But they'll need sun cream, of course.

James: OK. Thanks mum, that sounds good.

Dear friends _____

_____

When: _____

Where: _____

Please bring: _____

_____

_____

James

SB → p.104

1 **Email**

Du hast diese E-Mail von deinem britischen Austauschpartner Mohammed erhalten.
- Antworte ihm auf Englisch und gehe dabei auf seine E-Mail ein.
- Stelle ihm auch Fragen.

Schreibe eine E-Mail von ungefähr 100 Wörtern.

Hi there!

I'm looking forward to coming to your town on the school exchange.

I wanted to ask you about your town. What is it like? What is there for young people to do in the town? And what is there for tourists? Do you like your town, and why – or why not?

Please tell me about your family too. I'm looking forward to meeting them.

Bye for now
Mohammed

SB → p.105

2 **Picture and prompts**

Schreibe eine Geschichte auf Englisch, in der du das Bild und die Angaben berücksichtigst. Schreibe ungefähr 100 Wörter.
Beginne wie folgt:

The lost dog
Last Sunday morning Sophie and Tom went cycling in the country...

Mädchen in Tränen • ins Gespräch vertieft • Suche nach dem Hund • glückliches Ende

SB → p.105

1 👥 **Picture based interview PARTNER A** *(PARTNER B: Go to page 60)*

a Look at the picture below for about 30 seconds.
Then answer Partner B's questions. Talk for three minutes.

b Look at Partner B's picture. Ask three questions from Set A and two questions from Set B.

Set A	Set B
• Describe what the boy is doing. • Describe where the boy is. • Talk about the background. • Describe the boy. • What's the weather like?	• Why do you think the boy has come here? • What do people usually do in a park near you? • What are the downsides of mobiles for teens? • What can you do on your smartphone? • How often do you use your smartphone?

SB → *p.106*

2 👥 **Topic-based talk PARTNER A**
Your topic is 'New Zealand'. Talk about <u>three</u> of the six aspects below.
You can prepare and make notes if you wish. Then talk to Partner B for about two minutes.

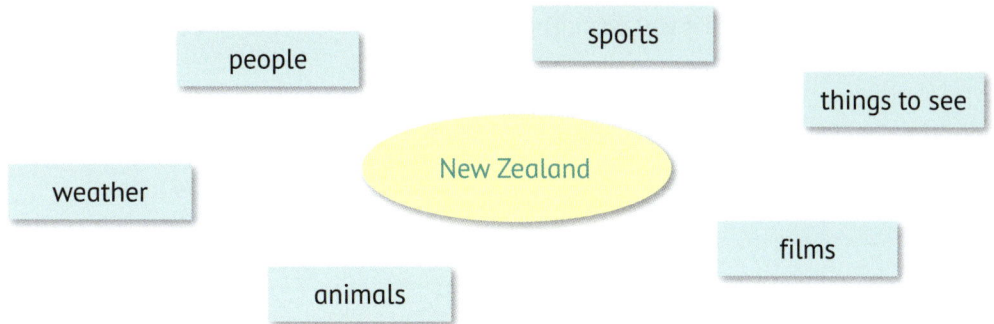

people

sports

things to see

New Zealand

weather

films

animals

SB → *p.107*

1 👥 **Picture based interview PARTNER B**

a Look at Partner A's picture. Ask three questions from Set A and two questions from Set B.

Set A	Set B
• Describe where the girls are.	• Who do you think the girls are?
• Describe what the girls are doing.	• What do you think they're saying?
• What can you see in the background?	• What is the living room like in your house?
• Describe the clothes.	• What do you like doing in your free time and why?
• What do the girls look like?	• What things do you do with members of your family?

b Look at the picture below for about 30 seconds.
Then answer Partner A's questions. Talk for three minutes.

SB → p.106

2 👥 **Topic-based talk PARTNER B**
Your topic is 'money'. Talk about <u>three</u> of the six aspects below.
You can prepare and make notes if you wish. Then talk to Partner A for about two minutes.

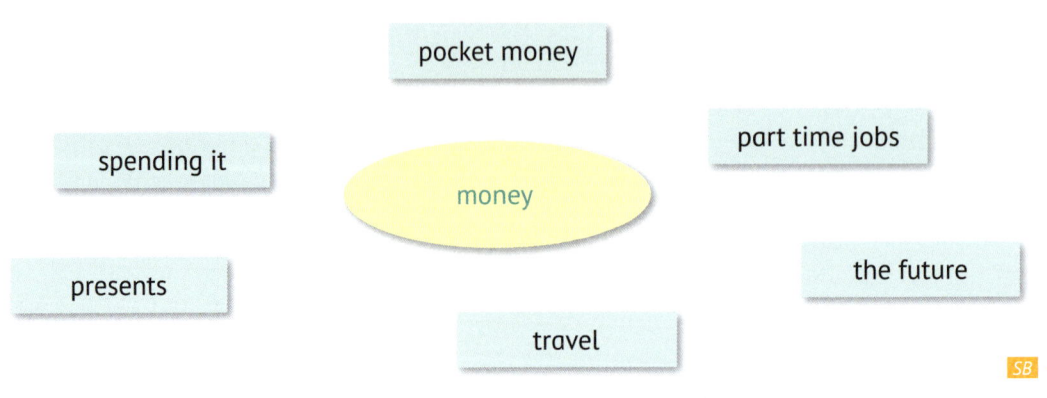

SB → p.107

infinitive	simple past	past participle	
(to) be	he/she/it **was** you/we/you/they **were**	been	sein
(to) become	became	become	werden
(to) bet	bet	bet	wetten
(to) begin	began	begun	beginnen, anfangen
(to) break	broke	broken	(zer)brechen; kaputtgehen/-machen
(to) bring	brought	brought	bringen, mitbringen
(to) build	built	built	(er)bauen
(to) buy	bought	bought	kaufen
(to) catch	caught	caught	(ein)fangen; erwischen
(to) come	came	come	(mit)kommen
(to) cost	cost	cost	kosten
(to) cut	cut	cut	schneiden; (Rasen) mähen
(to) do	did	done [ʌ]	machen, tun
(to) drink	drank	drunk	trinken
(to) drive	drove	driven	fahren (mit dem Auto)
(to) eat	ate [et, eɪt]	eaten	essen; fressen
(to) fall	fell	fallen	fallen; hinfallen
(to) feed	fed	fed	füttern
(to) feel	felt	felt	sich fühlen; fühlen
(to) fight	fought	fought	kämpfen
(to) find	found	found	finden
(to) fly	flew	flown	fliegen
(to) forget	forgot	forgotten	vergessen
(to) get	got	got	bekommen, kriegen
(to) give	gave	given	geben
(to) go	went	gone [ɒ]	gehen; fahren
(to) grow	grew	grown	wachsen; werden
(to) have	had	had	haben
(to) hear [ɪə]	heard [ɜː]	heard [ɜː]	hören
(to) hit	hit	hit	schlagen; stoßen; treffen
(to) hold	held	held	halten
(to) keep	kept	kept	behalten
(to) know [nəʊ]	knew [njuː]	known [nəʊn]	wissen; kennen
(to) leave	left	left	verlassen; zurücklassen; abfahren
(to) lose	lost	lost	verlieren
(to) lie	lay	lain	liegen
(to) make	made	made	machen, herstellen
(to) mean	meant	meant	bedeuten; meinen, sagen wollen
(to) meet	met	met	kennenlernen; (sich) treffen; abholen
(to) pay	paid	paid	(be)zahlen
(to) put	put	put	stellen, legen, (etwas wohin) tun
(to) read [iː]	read [e]	read [e]	lesen
(to) ride [aɪ]	rode	ridden [ɪ]	reiten; (Rad) fahren
(to) ring	rang	rung	läuten, klingeln
(to) run	ran	run	rennen
(to) say [eɪ]	said [e]	said [e]	sagen
(to) see	saw	seen	sehen
(to) sell	sold	sold	verkaufen
(to) send	sent	sent	schicken, senden (an)
(to) teach	taught	taught	unterrichten; lehren
(to) tell	told	told	erzählen, sagen
(to) think	thought	thought	denken, meinen, glauben
(to) understand	understood	understood	verstehen
(to) wake	woke	woken	wecken
(to) wear [eə]	wore [ɔː]	worn [ɔː]	tragen, anhaben (Kleidung)
(to) win	won	won	gewinnen
(to) write [aɪ]	wrote	written [ɪ]	schreiben

LISTENING

1 **Declan's birthday**
1 *b* 2 *c* 3 *a* 4 *a snake* 5 *d* 6 *10.30 / half past ten*

2 **Samira's terrible day**
1 ~~mum's~~ *dad's* 2 ~~sunny~~ *raining* 3 ~~car~~ *bus* 4 ~~hand~~ *leg* 5 ~~was~~ *wasn't* 6 ~~lesson~~ *test*

3 **A phone message**
1 *the garage* 2 *ZH65GCW* 3 *the engine* 4 *order a new part* 5 *724 691* 6 *end of the week*

USE OF ENGLISH

1 **A tour with a difference**
1 ~~who~~ *what* 2 ~~at~~ *in* 3 ~~taking~~ *take* 4 ~~much~~ *many* 5 ~~who~~ *that / which*
6 ~~were living~~ *lived* 7 ~~as~~ *like* 8 ~~interested~~ *interesting*

2 **Hobbies**
In your last email you *asked* me if I liked reading. Yes, I *do*. I usually read about two or three books *every/per* week. My favourite books are crime novels – I love them because they're so *exciting*. What *sort/kind/type* of books do you like? I like *watching* crime series on TV too. *What* about you? What are your favourite programmes? *Are* there any British crime programmes on German TV? Have you *ever* read any crime novels by British writers?

3 **Advice from friends**
1 *B* 2 *A* 3 *C* 4 *B* 5 *D* 6 *C* 7 *B* 8 *D*

READING

1 **An article in a school magazine**
1 *G* 2 *D* 3 *F* 4 *C* 5 *A* 6 *E*

2 **Saving lives at sea**
1 *nearly 180 years* 2 *saves lives at sea* 3 *more than 140,000*
4 *346* 5 *none / nothing* 6 *stormy winds and fog*

MEDIATION

1 **A part time job**
(sample answer) Am besten singst du Lieder, die beliebt und familienfreundlich sind.

Gute Orte für Straßenmusik sind Einkaufsstraßen und gute Zeiten sind samstags oder in der Mittagszeit.

Es kann sein, dass du eine besondere Genehmigung brauchst.

Du solltest vorher gut üben, denn wenn du nicht gut bist, bekommst du kein Geld. Nimm Rücksicht auf andere: Singe nicht zu laut und bleibe nicht zu lange am gleichen Ort. Wenn es kalt ist, solltest du dich warm anziehen. Falls jemand blöde Sprüche macht, lass dich nicht stressen. Du kannst auch mit Jonglieren, Akrobatik, Tanzen oder Pantomime auf der Straße Geld verdienen.

2 **A fitness tracker**

Was der Fitness Tracker kann	· Er sagt dir, wie lange und wie gut du geschlafen hast. · Er sagt dir, wenn du zu lange gesessen hast. · Er ist wasserdicht / du kannst damit ins Wasser gehen.
Batterie	· Die Batterie hält für ungefähr 12 Tage, wenn das GPS eingeschaltet ist nur für 4 Stunden.
Was ist nicht so gut?	· Die Bedienungsanleitung ist nicht sonderlich gut. · Wenn die Sonne scheint, ist das Display schwer zu lesen.

TEXT- UND MEDIENKOMPETENZEN

Birthday invitation
Dear friends
Please come / You are invited to my birthday party.
When: Saturday, 13th June, 3.30pm
Where: At the swimming pool
Please bring: food and drink, swimming costume,
towel, suncream
I hope you can come!
James

WRITING

1 **Email**

(sample answer) Hi Mohammed

Thanks for your email. You asked about my town.

It's quite big and modern, but the town centre is old. There are a lot of things for young people, for example you can go bowling or skating and there's a good cinema. We have an interesting museum for tourists, and you can go on a boat trip on the river.

I like the town because it's always busy and there are things to do, but everything is expensive.

I live with my mum and my sister. Mum works in a bank, and my sister is seven and she's called Nora.

I'm looking forward to seeing you.

Bye for now

2 **Picture and prompts**

(sample answer) Last Sunday morning Sophie and Tom went cycling in the country. Suddenly, they saw a girl. She was crying.

"Why are you crying?" asked Sophie.

"I've lost my dog," said the girl. "He ran away and I don't know where he is."

There were two roads, so Tom asked "Which way did he go?"

"I don't know," answered the girl.

"Don't worry. We'll look for him," said Sophie. "We can go fast on our bikes."

She went along one road and Tom went along the other one. Twenty minutes later, they came back with the dog.

"Thank you so much!" said the girl.